I0606120

Helen Roseveare

What's in the Parcel?

The true story of Helen Roseveare and the hot water bottle

Catherine Mackenzie
Illustrated by Rita Ammassari

In the little church, Christmas carols were being sung and a sense of excitement was in the air. The snow was falling outside. Helen shivered a little and cuddled up to her mother. Winter was cold in England.

But her heart felt warm as she thought about the Christmas stockings and parcels that would soon be in their living room ... along with the brand new baby sister that had just been born.

In the little church Christmas carols were being sung.

As she knelt in the quiet little church, Helen heard the words, 'Christ died for you.'

Many years later, Helen realised that these words were true. Jesus Christ had died for her. Her sins were forgiven. After she had finished her medical studies at university, she knew that she wanted to go to Africa. There wasn't any snow there. Not many people knew about Christmas. Very few had ever heard of Jesus.

It would be hard work, but she knew that God would help her. She could trust in him ... for anything.

Helen heard the words 'Christ died for you.'

Late one night in the African hospital, Helen could hear a little girl sobbing and a newborn baby crying. A young mother had just died.

The hospital would have to look after the children now, but there was no electricity and the night was getting very cold. Helen knew it would be difficult to keep the baby alive. She sent for a hot water bottle. They must keep the baby warm.

Helen knew it would be difficult to keep the baby alive.

But the last hot water bottle had burst. What could they do? Helen couldn't buy another one. There weren't any shops. She couldn't phone to get one delivered – their village was right in the middle of the jungle. So Helen did the best she could.

She told a nurse, 'Put the baby as near the fire as you can. Try and keep it away from the drafts. Your job is to keep the baby warm.'

Helen did the best she could.

The following day, Helen went to visit the orphans and told them about the little girl and the baby. She explained about how difficult it was to keep the baby warm. 'We need a hot water bottle,' she told the children. 'The baby might die if it gets chilled.'

Helen went to visit the orphans.

Just then, a ten-year-old girl called Ruth decided to pray to God about the problem. ‘Please God,’ she prayed, ‘send us a hot water bottle. It’ll be no good tomorrow God, the baby will be dead, so please send it this afternoon. And while you are about it, would you please send a dolly for the little girl so she’ll know you really love her.’

Ruth decided to pray to God.

Helen was astonished. Would God really answer this prayer? God could do everything, but would God really send them a hot water bottle and a doll just like that? Nobody would ever think of sending a hot water bottle to Africa – one of the hottest places in the world!

Would God really send them a hot water bottle and a doll?

Halfway through the afternoon, a car arrived at Helen's front door. Helen went to see who it was, but by the time she got there the car had gone. However, on the doorstep there was a large parcel! Helen couldn't believe her eyes. Quickly she sent for the orphanage children and together they carefully opened the parcel.

On the doorstep there was a large parcel.

Lots of little eyes focused on the large cardboard box. Helen pulled out some brightly knitted jerseys. Then, there were bandages for the patients. Next, came a box of raisins. Helen put her hand in once again and stopped. Could it really be? Yes. It was! A brand-new rubber, hot water bottle!

Helen put her hand in once again and stopped.

Helen had not asked God to send it. Ruth had and it was Ruth who rushed forward, crying out, 'If God has sent the bottle, he must have sent the dolly too!' Rummaging down to the bottom of the box, she pulled out the small, beautifully dressed dolly.

Ruth's eyes shone: she had never doubted! Looking up at Helen she asked, 'Can I give this dolly to that little girl, so she'll know that Jesus really loves her?'

Ruth's eyes shone.

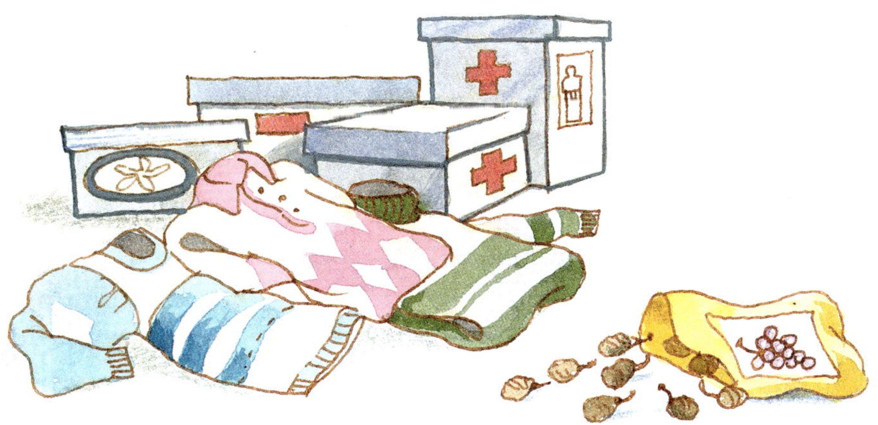

That parcel had been packed up by Helen's former Sunday School class five months earlier. Ruth had prayed that afternoon – and God had answered.

'And it shall come to pass, that before they call, I will answer; and while they are yet speaking, I will hear.' (Isaiah 65:24)

God had answered.

For Lydia, Esther, Philip, Lois, Jack, Marianne and Isobel
Christ Jesus died for you!

ISBN: 978-1-84550-383-3
Reprinted 2012, 2014, 2016, 2020, 2022 and 2025

Published by Christian Focus Publications
Geanies House, Fearn, Tain, Ross-shire, IV20 1TW,
Scotland, U.K.
www.christianfocus.com

Illustrated by Rita Ammassari
Cover design by Daniel van Straaten
Printed and bound by Imprint, India